DAY TRADING

CRASH COURSE

THE CRASH COURSE FOR FOREX MARKET AND
OPTIONS TRADING STRATEGIES.
ADVANCED TACTICS FOR DAY TRADING

Andrew Elder

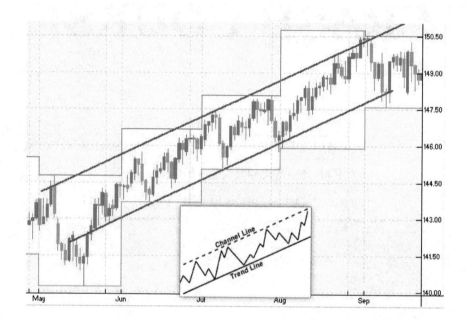

original author of this work can be in any fashion deemed liable for any hardship or damages that may befall them after undertaking the information described herein.

Additionally, the information in the following pages is intended only for informational purposes and should thus be thought of as universal. As befitting its nature, it is presented without assurance regarding its prolonged validity or interim quality. Trademarks that are mentioned are done without written consent and can in no way be considered an endorsement from the trademark holder.

TABLE OF CONTENTS

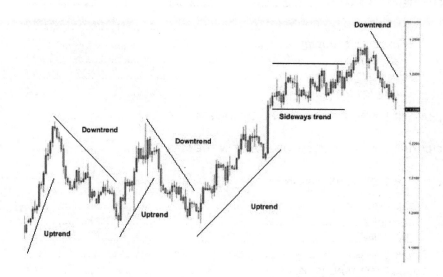

Introduction

It is essential that you understand and apply all these three elements in day trading. While some strategies only require technical indicators (like VWAP and Moving Average), it will help you a lot if you understand price action and chart patterns, so you can be a profitable day trader.

This knowledge, especially about price action comes only with regular practice. As a day trader, you must not care about the company and its revenue. You should not be distracted by the mission or vision of the company or how much money they make. Your focus must only be on the chart patterns, technical indicators, and price action.

Successful day traders also don't mix technical analysis with fundamental analysis. Day traders usually focus more on technical analysis.

The catalyst is the reason why a particular stock is running. If you have a stock that is running up to 70%, you need to determine the catalyst behind this change, and never stop until you figure that one out.

So, it's a tech company that just got patent approval or a pharmaceutical company that passed through important clinical trials. These are catalysts that can help you understand what is really going on.

Beyond this, don't bother yourself squinting over revenue papers or listening in conference calls. You should not care about these things unless you are a long-term investor.

Day traders trade fast. There are times that you may find yourself trading in time periods as short as 10 to 30 seconds, and can make thousands of dollars. If the market is moving fast, you need to make certain that you are in the right position to take advantage of the profits and minimize your risk exposure.

There are millions of day traders out there with different strategies. Each trader requires its strategy and edge. You must find your spot in the market whenever you feel comfortable.

You must focus on day trading strategies because these really work for day trading. The following strategies have been proven effective in day trading. These strategies are quite basic in theory, but they can be challenging to master and requires a lot of practice.

Also remember that in the market today, more than 60% of the volume is dominated by algorithmic trading. So you are really competing against computers. There's a big chance that you will lose against an algorithm. You may get lucky a couple of times, but supercomputers will win the game.

Trading stocks against computers means that the majority of the changes in stocks that you see are the result of computers moving shares around. On one hand, it also means that there are certain stocks every day that will be traded on such heavy retail volume.

Every day, you have to focus on trading these specific stocks or the Apex Predators - the stocks that are usually gapping down or up on revenue.

You should hunt for stocks that have considerable interest among day traders and considerable retail volume. These are the stocks that you can buy, and together, the retail traders can still win the game against algorithmic traders.

One principle in day trading that you may find useful is that you must only choose the setups that you want to master. Using basic trading methods that are composed of minimal setups is effective in reducing the stress and confusion, and will allow you to focus more on the psychological effect of trading. This will separate the losers from the winners.

Managing Your Day Trades

It is always intriguing when two-day traders choose the same stock - the one short and the other long.

More often than not, both traders become profitable, proving that trader management and experience are more important than the stock and the strategy used by the trader.

Remember, your trade size will depend on the price of the stock and your account and risk management. Beginners in day trading is recommended to limit the size of their shares below 1000.

For example, you can buy 800 shares, then sell half in the first target. You can bring your stop loss to break even. Then you can sell another 200 in the next target. You can keep the last 200 shares until you stop. You can always maintain some shares in case the price will keep on moving in your favor.

IMPORTANT: Professional day traders never risk their shares all at once.

They know how to scale into the trade, which means they buy shares at different points. They may start with 200 shares and then add to their position in different steps. For instance, for an 800-share trader, they could enter either 400/400 or 100/200/500 shares. When done properly, this is an excellent way to manage your trades and risks. But managing the position in the system can be overly difficult. Many newbies who may attempt to do this could end up over trading and may lose their money in slippage, commissions, and averaging down the losing stocks. Rare is the chance that you may scale into a trade. Still, there are times that you can do this, especially in high-volume trades.

However, you should take note that scaling into a trade

increases your risk and beginners can use it improperly as a way to average down their losing positions. We have discussed this for the sake of information, and this is not recommended for beginners.

Even though they may appear the same, there's a big difference between averaging down a losing position and scaling into a trade. For newbies, averaging down a losing position can wipe out your account, especially with small accounts that are not strong enough for averaging down.

ABCD Pattern

The ABCD Pattern is the simplest pattern you can trade, and this is an ideal choice for amateur day traders. Even though this is pretty much basic and has been used by day traders for a long time, it still works quite effectively because many day traders are still using it.

This pattern has a self-fulfilling prophecy effect, so you just follow the trend.

The chart above shows an example of an ABCD pattern in the stock market. This one begins with a strong upwards move. Buyers are quickly buying stocks as represented by point A, and making new highs in point B. In this trend, you may choose to enter the trade, but you must not be overly obsessed with the trade, because, at point B, it can be quite extended and at its highest price.

Moreover, you can't ascertain the stop for this pattern. Take note that you should never enter a trade without identifying your stop. At point B, traders who purchased the stock earlier begin gradually selling it for profit and the prices will also come down.

Still, you must not enter the trade because you are not certain where the bottom of this trend will be. But if you see that the price doesn't come down from a specific level such as point C, it means that the stock has discovered possible support.

Thus, you can plan your trade and set up the stops and a point to take the profits.

For example, OPTT (Ocean Power Technologies Inc) announced in 2016 that they closed a new $50 million deal. This one is a good example of a fundamental catalyst. OPTT stocks surged from $7.70 (Point A) to $9.40 (B) at around 9 am. Day traders who were not aware of the news waited for point B and then an indication that the stock will not go lower than a specific price (C).

If you saw that C holds support and buyers are fighting back to allow the stock price to go any lower than the price at C, you will know that the price will be higher. Buyers jumped on massively.

Remember, the ABCD Pattern is a basic day trading strategy, and many retail traders are looking for it. Near point D, the volume immediately spiked, which means that the traders are now in the trade. When the stock made a new low, it was a clear exit signal.

Here are the specific steps you can follow to use the ABCD strategy:

1. Whenever you see that a stock is surging up from point A and about to reach a new high for the day (point B), then wait to see if the price makes support higher than A. You can mark this as point C, but don't jump right into it.

2. Monitor the stock during its consolidation phase, then choose your share size and plan your stop and exit.

3. If you see that the price is holding support at point C, then you can participate in the trade closer to the price point C to anticipate the move to point D or even higher.

4. Your stop could be at C. When the price goes lower than C, you can sell. Thus, it is crucial to buy the stock closer to C to reduce the loss. (Some day traders have a higher tolerance, so they wait a bit more near D to ensure that the ABCD pattern is complete. However, this is risky as it can reduce your profit).

5. When the price moves higher, you can sell half of your shares near point D, and bring your stop higher to your breakeven point.

6. Sell the rest of your shares as soon as you hit your target or you feel that the price is losing momentum, or that the sellers are getting control of the price action.

Bull Flag Momentum

Expert stock analysts consider the Bull Flag Momentum as a scalping strategy because the flags in the pattern don't usually last long. Plus, day traders should scalp the trade to get in quickly, make money, and then exit the market.

Below is an example of a Bull Flag pattern with one notable consolidation.

This chart is called Bull Flag because it is like a flag on a pole. In this pattern, you have different large candles rising (pole) and you also have a sequence of small candles that move sideways (flag) or "consolidating" in day trading jargon.

When there is consolidation in the pattern, it signifies that traders who purchased the stocks at a lower price are now selling.

While this is happening, the price doesn't significantly decrease because buyers are still participating in the trades, and sellers are not yet in control of the price. Many retail traders will miss buying the stock before the Bull Flag begins. Buying stocks when the price is increasing could be risky. This is known as "chasing the stock". Successful day traders usually aim to participate in the trade during quiet periods and take their profits during wild periods.

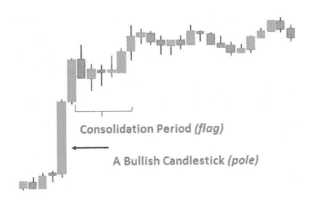

Consolidation Period *(flag)*

A Bullish Candlestick *(pole)*

Chapter 1

Breakout

Break out is known to be one of the most straightforward approaches to use in forex trading. It is easy to note when you are wrong. You can tell when the price goes higher in the range or lower your range. Break up is defined either by the swing high or swing lows or characterized by support or resistance. Swing low is a mini version of support and resistance. They are not of significance, but they are pretty evident on the chats when you identify swing highs or lows in the market. Resistance in the market is where there will be potential sellers coming into the market. Resistance is much more respectable and is vary obviously in your chat.

There is a period that you should avoid trading breakouts. You need to know that you should not trade breakouts against the trends as you know that the trend is not your "friend" until it bends. It is not much you can gain if you are trading against the trend. You should also not trade breakouts when the market is far much from the stricture. The problem of going longs in the structure is that you will never know where to put your stop loss as there will know structure to guide you.

To trade breakouts like a pro, you need to:

- Trade with the trend
- Trade near the stricture
- Trade breakouts with the buildups. Buildups are the congested area in your chat where the sellers are not making any pressure. Maybe it is due to sellers not being there, or there are a good number of buyers who are willing to buy at higher prices. These are signs of strengths that you need to look up to.

Breakout Strategy

This is a common strategy employed by traders new and old. The main idea behind this strategy is that you chose a price point for a given stock that, once hit, will indicate enough of a positive swing to justify buying more of the stock. When using this method, it is important to consider a price point as well as the amount of time you are willing to give the stock for it to reach that price point. This is a strong strategy to employ if the market is moving in a certain direction and ensures you will always know when to jump on the bandwagon.

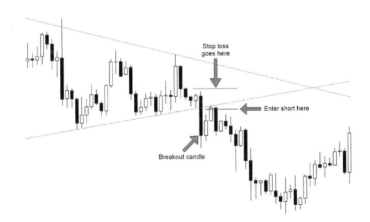

This strategy is an effective choice if the market is currently or was recently at either a drastic high or low. To complete this strategy properly, all you need to do is set an order that is either above the high or slightly above the low and then play the averages. If the market is not moving strongly in one direction or another, then this strategy can easily backfire as prices are more likely to stick to prescribed ranges. If there are no strong signs of trending use caution.

Retracement strategy

To properly implement this strategy, you must be able to determine a likely pattern for the price of the stock to continue trending towards. To take advantage of this fact, you wait for each price increase before the inevitable decrease which comes as some people sell and others try and trade the opposite. You sell on the high and use the profits to buy back in at an increase of shares under the assumption that it will rise again. Then you simply repeat until you are no longer sure of the increase.

This strategy will only work effectively when there is something major enough to cause ripples across the market that are not felt all at once. This strategy will become less effective the unsure you are about additional jumps in price and should therefore always be used carefully. You may be tempted after seeing a single large jump from stock to try

and employ this strategy but beware of using it flippantly. Stay strong and you will turn a profit.

Pivot points

In order to take advantage of this strategy, it is important that you first become extremely familiar with the specific securities that you prefer to work with day in and day out so that you have a general understanding of their high and low points, thus making it easier to predict where it is likely they are going to go next.

If you don't have access to this type of first-hand information, then you can use existing historical charts to make do, as long as you can clearly determine the highs and lows for the security in question. In order to ensure this strategy works as well as possible, you will need to have a clear top and bottom determination. You will then simply buy or sell based on not where the security is currently going, but where it is likely to go once it rounds the pivot point and starts back the other way.

Essentially, you are going to look at these charts and try to figure out where the lowest and the highest points are. When the stock gets to the lowest point, it is time to enter the market and purchase the stock at a lower price, hopefully, lower than market value. You will then hold onto the stock for a bit, waiting for it to reach the high point on the chart, or at least

higher than where you started so that you can make a profit when it's time to sell.

Pairs trading

As the name implies, pairs trading is a strategy wherein you choose a general category of stocks, tech stocks, for example, and then go short on one stock in the sector while going long on the other. Making these trades at the same time will bolster your odds of ensuring one of them actually turns a profit while also ensuring that you can turn a profit regardless of the conditions in the market. You will also be able to see movement on all sides more easily including sideways movement, downtrends, and uptrends and then bet on a few different options within the market. Since you are betting on both sides, you are more likely to make some money compared to just picking one kind of stock.

Contrarian trading

Day traders that use momentum to trade will buy bonds and stocks when their prices are going up and selling them when the prices begin to go down. These people believe that if something is going up in its price, it will continue to do so for a while and that something that is falling will continue to fall. Momentum trading is only one trading strategy, and, for most traders, it works well, especially with a strong bull market. Contrarian trading, though, is the exact opposite of those momentum traders and it also can work very

well. The belief in the contrarian strategy is that things aren't going to continue to rise forever and that nothing will fall forever.

The contrarian investment style goes against the market trends that are currently prevailing by purchasing assets that are performing poorly, and sell them once they are performing well. This type of investor believes that when another person says that the market is moving up, does so when they are completely invested and aren't planning on purchasing more. This means the market is at its peak, which means a downturn is about to happen, and the contrarian investor has already sold.

A trader that uses the contrarian strategy will look for assets that have been on the rise and will sell them, and they prefer to buy stocks that have been falling in price. It doesn't mean that you should buy cheap or sell but instead look for things that appear to be overpriced and to buy what looks to be a bargain. Contrarian investment also emphasizes out-of-favor securities that have a low P/E ratio.

This investment style is distinguished from others in that they buy and sell against the grain of what other investors believe at a given time. These investors will enter the market when others feel pessimistic about it, and its value is a lot lower than the intrinsic value. When there is such a largely pessimistic view about a stock, the chances of the price lowering so low that the risks and downfalls of the stock are overblown.

Finding out which of the distressed stocks to purchase and then sell it after the company has recovered will boost the value of the stock. This is the main play of the contrarian investor.

Chapter 2

Application on the Options Market

Very successful investor says that research makes all the difference not only in options trading but trading in general. The better resources you have the more knowledge you will acquire. This is especially significant for learning as much as you can about underlying securities for example or to find as many details about the market that is constantly changing. Significance of the right source of information eventually becomes the key to your progress, even more, if the world of options trading is still new to you. We can say that there are two types of relevant resources for options trading. The first one includes traditional resources such as magazines, newsletters, and newspapers. The second type is newer, it has a variety of options and these kinds of resources are mostly referred to as online resources.

The Internet offers a variety of free content, which is why

many investors see it as their first stop whenever they need some kind of information. Further technology development also had a huge impact on the amount of information, tools, and possibilities that a person can access so using apps for education and trading, in general, has become a common thing. In the following text, we will list some of the most relevant option trading resources divided into the categories we explained above.

Even though they are considered to be more traditional, magazines, newspapers, newsletters, are still popular for research, for both experienced investors and beginners on the market. It is useful to know that many newsletters offer paid services such as recommendations, picks, research of certain categories, and other relevant information.

We will start with the magazines. Some of them such as Forbes are still one of the greatest and strongest magazines in the world for this matter. So, we have Fortune, Forbes, Consumer Money Adviser, Bloomberg BusinessWeek, Kiplinger's, and Fast Company as some of the most relevant magazines today. Newspapers that you might find useful are the Financial Times, the Wall Street Journal, The Washington Post, Value Line, and Barron's.

Some of the most recommended ones are ETF Trader, Market Watch Options Trader, The Proactive Fund Investor, Hulbert Interactive, The Technical Indicator, The Prudent Speculator,

Dow Theory Forecasts, and Global Resources Trading

When it comes to online resources, they are probably the most frequent source of information for everything, not only for options trading. However, it is possible to find numerous websites that offer research that is up to date. Many of these analyses and other useful data can be found for free.

Technology development made many things easier with trading. Many apps have emerged and enabled investors to keep a close track of their investments at all times. It is important to know that there are apps that are not only for investment but for brokerage companies too. In the following text, you can find some of the investment apps that are most frequently used and that have excellent feedback.

How to avoid costly mistakes

Losing profit is not something that you want as an investor since the main purpose of options trading is to make money not the other way around. To do so, some tips can help you avoid mistakes that can be costly.

First of all, don't invest more capital than you are ready to lose. Keep in mind that trading options don't go without risks. There aren't any guarantees that the propositions that you'll face will gain you anything and your decisions are based on the hunch. Furthermore, if you don't have good timing and

your hunch isn't right, you can lose the entire investment, not only the cash you were expecting to earn. The best way to avoid this kind of scenario is to start small. It is recommended that you use no more than 15 percent of your total portfolio on options trading.

The second tip that you should be aware of at all times is that good research gets the job done. If somebody says that it is a good idea to invest in options and you rush in and make an order without thinking it through, once more, you can lose more than you could earn. You should make your research and decide based on facts before you start trading.

There is another thing that you should be mindful of. No matter the strategy you choose for options trading, you should always try to adjust it to the current condition on the market. Not all strategies work in all environments which is why you must be up to date with circumstances in the world of finance and you have to adapt accordingly.

Without a proper exit strategy, it is useless to talk about successful business in options trading. You need to make a plan that you will follow through regardless of your emotions. Rational decisions are the main factor in trade, being emotional and making fast decisions out of rage or spite or feeling of insecurity can only make things worse. Stick to the plan you figured before you started trading because it should have both downside and upside points along with the

timeframe for its execution. Just like you shouldn't let negative feelings influence your decision-making, you shouldn't allow the feeling of over-confidence in gaining large profits to pull you back from the path you have set for yourself. When it comes to risks, there is no need to take more risks than necessary, which means that the level of risk should be as big as your comfort with it. Level of risk tolerance is different for everyone; it is an individual think and only the investor himself can set its limit. Try to estimate that level and then choose all further actions accordingly. It is the safest premise to base your decisions on without being too insecure about every choice you make.

Chapter 3

Analyzing Mood Swing in the Market

The market is a chaotic place with several traders vying for dominance over one another. There is a countless number of strategies and time frames in play and at any point, it is close to impossible to determine who will emerge with the upper hand. In such an environment, how is it then possible to make any money? After all, if everything is unpredictable, how can you get your picks right?

Well, this is where thinking in terms of probabilities comes into play. While you cannot get every single bet right, as long as you get enough right and make enough money on those to offset your losses, you will make money in the long run.

It's not about getting one or two right. It's about executing the strategy with the best odds of winning over and over again and ensuring that your math works out with regards to the relationship between your win rate and average win.

So, it really comes down to finding patterns that repeat themselves over time in the markets. What causes these patterns? Well, the other traders of course! To put it more accurately, the orders that the other traders place in the market are what create patterns that repeat themselves over time.

The first step to understanding these patterns is to understand what trends and ranges are. Identifying them and learning to spot when they transition into one another will give you a massive leg up not only with your options trading but also with directional trading.

Trends

In theory spotting, a trend is simple enough. Look left to right and if the price is headed up or down, it's a trend. Well, sometimes it is really that simple. However, for the majority of the time you have both with and counter-trend forces operating in the market. It is possible to have long counter-trend reactions within a larger trend and sometimes, depending on the time frame you're in, these counter-trend reactions take up the majority of your screen space.

Trend vs. Range

This is a chart of the UK100 CFD, which mimics the FTSE 100, on the four-hour time frame. Three-quarters of the chart is a downtrend and the last quarter are a wild uptrend. Using the looking left to a right guideline, we'd conclude that this instrument is in a range. Is that really true though?

Just looking at that chart, you can clearly see that short-term momentum is bullish. So, if you were considering taking a trade on this, would you implement a range strategy or a trending one? This is exactly the sort of thing that catches traders up.

The key to deciphering trends is to watch for two things: counter-trend participation quality and turning points. Let's tackle counter-trend participation first.

Counter Trend Participation

When a new trend begins, the market experiences an extremely imbalanced order flow that is tilted towards one side. There's isn't much counter-trend participation against this seeming tidal wave of with trend orders. Price marches on without any opposition and experiences only a few hiccups.

As time goes on though, the trend forces run out of steam and have to take breaks to gather themselves. This is where counter-trend traders start testing the trend and trying to see how far back into the trend they can go. While it is unrealistic to expect a full reversal at this point, the quality of the correction or pushback tells us a lot about the strength distribution between the with and counter-trend forces.

Eventually, the counter-trend players manage to push so far back against the trend that a stalemate results in the market. The counter-trend forces are equally balanced and thus the trend comes to an end. After all, you need an imbalance for the market to tip one way or another and a balanced order flow is only going to result in a sideways market.

While all this is going on behind the scenes, the price chart is what records the push and pull between these two forces. Using the price chart, we can not only anticipate when a trend is coming to an end but also how long it could potentially take before it does. This second factor, which helps us estimate the time it could take, is invaluable from an options perspective, especially if you're using a horizontal spread strategy.

In all cases, the greater the number of them, the greater the counter-trend participation in the market. The closer a trend is to end, the greater the counter-trend participation. Thus, the minute you begin to see price move into a large, sideways move with an equal number of buyers and sellers in it, you can be sure that some form of redistribution is going on.

Mind you, the trend might continue or reverse. Either way, it doesn't matter. What matters is that you know the trend is weak and that now is probably not the time to be banking on-trend strategies.

Starting from the left, we can see that there are close to no counter-trend bars, bearish in this case, and the bulls make easy progress. Note the angle with which the bulls proceed upwards.

Then comes the first major correction and the counter-trend players push back against the last third of the bull move. Notice how strong the bearish bars are and note their character compared to the bullish bars.

The bulls recover and push the price higher at the original angle and without any bearish presence, which seems odd. This is soon explained as the bears' slam price back down and for a while, it looks as if they've managed to form a V top reversal in the trend, which is an extremely rare occurrence.

The price action that follows is a more accurate reflection of the power in the market, with both bulls and bears sharing chunks of the order flow, with overall order flow in the bull's favor but only just. Price here is certainly in an uptrend but looking at the extent of the bearish pushbacks, perhaps we should be on our guard for a bearish reversal. After all order flow is looking pretty sideways at this point.

So how would we approach an options strategy with the chart in the state it is in at the extreme right? Well, for one, any strategy that requires an option beyond the near month is out of the question, given the probability of it turning. Secondly, looking at the order flow, it does seem to be following a channel, doesn't it?

While the channel isn't very clean, if you were aggressive enough, you could consider deploying a collar with the strike prices above and below this channel to take advantage of the price movement. You could also employ some moderately bullish strategies as price approaches the bottom of this channel and figuring out the extent of the bull move is easier thanks to you being able to reference the top of the channel.

As price moves in this channel, it's all well and good. Eventually, though, we know that the trend has to flip. How do we know when this happens?

Turning Points

As bulls and bears struggle over who gets to control the order flow, price swings up and down. You will notice that every time price comes back into the 6427-6349 zone, the bulls seem to step in masse and repulse the bears.

This tells us that the bulls are willing to defend this level in large numbers and strongly at that. Given the number of times the bears have tested this level, we can safely assume that above this level, bullish strength is a bit weak. However, at this level, it is as if the bulls have retreated and are treating this as a sort of last resort, for the trend to be maintained. You can see where I'm going with this.

If this level were to be breached by the bears, it is a good bet that a large number of bulls will be taken out. In martial terms, the largest army of bulls has been marshaled at this level. If this force is defeated, it is unlikely that there's going to be too much resistance to the bears below this level.

This zone, in short, is a turning point. If price breaches this zone decisively, we can safely assume that the bears have moved in and control the majority if the order flow.

Turning Point Breached

The decisive turning point zone is marked by the two horizontal lines and the price touches this level twice more and is repulsed by the bulls. Notice how the last bounce before the level breaks produces an extremely weak bullish bounce and price simply caves through this. Notice the strength with which the bears break through.

The FTSE was in a longer uptrend on the weekly chart, so the bulls aren't completely done yet. However, as far as the daily timeframe is concerned, notice how price retests that same level but this time around, it acts as resistance instead of support.

For now, we can conclude that as long as the price remains below the turning point, we are bearishly biased. You can see this by looking at the angle with which bulls push back as well as, the lack of strong bearish participation on the push upwards.

This doesn't mean we go ahead and pencil in a bull move and start implementing strategies that take advantage of the upcoming bullish move. Remember, nothing is for certain in the markets. Don't change your bias or strategy until the turning point decisively breaks.

Some key things to note here are that a turning point is always a major S/R level. It is usually a swing point where a large number of trend forces gather to support the trend. This will not always be the case, so don't make the mistake of hanging on to older turning points.

The current order flow and price action are what matters the most, so pay attention to that above all else. Also, note how the candles that test this level all have wicks on top of them.

This indicates that the bears are quite strong here and that any subsequent attack will be handled the same way until the level breaks. Do we know when the level will break? Well, we can't say with any accuracy. However, we can estimate the probability of it breaking.

The latest upswing has seen very little bearish pushback, comparatively speaking, and the push into the level is strong. Instinct would say that there's one more rejection left here. However, who knows? Until the level breaks, we stay bearish. When the level breaks, we switch to the bullish side.

Putting it all Together

So now we're ready to put all of this together into one coherent package. Your analysis should always begin with determining the current state of the market. Ranges are pretty straightforward to spot, and they occur either within big pullbacks in trends or at the end of trends.

Chapter 4

Options Trading Strategies

Options Strategies

We are now going to leave the world of selling options and go back to the one that most people are interested in, which is the world of trading options. We are going to have a look at strategies that can be used to increase the odds of profits when trading options. In reality, some of these strategies involve buying and selling options at the same time. Keep in mind that these techniques will require a higher-level designation from your broker. So, it might not be something you can use right away if you are a beginner.

Strangles

One of the simplest strategies that go beyond simply buying options, hoping to profit on moves of the underlying share price, is called a strangle. This strategy involves buying a call option and a put option simultaneously. They will have the same expiration dates, but different strike prices. If the price of the stock rises the put option will expire worthless (but of course it may still hold a small amount of value when you closed your position, and you can sell it and recoup some of the loss). But you will make a profit off the call option. On the other hand, if the stock price declines, the call option will expire worthlessly, but you can make a profit from the put option.

In this case, you can make substantial profits no matter which way the stock moves, but the larger the move, the more profits. On the upside, the profit potential is theoretically unlimited. On the downside, the stock could theoretically fall to zero, so there is a limit, but potential gains are substantial. The breakeven price on the upside is the strike price of the call plus the amount of the two premiums settled for the options. If the stock price declines the breakeven price would be the difference between the strike value of the put option and the sum of the two premiums paid for the options.

Straddles

When you purchase a call and a put option with similar strike amounts and expiration dates, this is called a straddle. The idea here is that the trader is hoping the share price will either rise or fall by a significant amount. It won't matter which way the price moves. Again, if the price rises the put option will expire worthless, if the price falls the call option will expire worthlessly. For example, suppose a stock is trading at $100 a share. We can buy at the money call and put options that expire in 30 days. The price of the call and put options would be $344 and $342 respectively, for a total investment of $686. With 20 days left to expiration, suppose the share price rises to $107. Then the call is priced at $766, and the put is at $65. We can sell them both at this time, for $831, and make a profit of $145.

Suppose that, instead of at 20 days to expiration, the share price dropped to $92. In that case, the call is priced at $39, and the put is priced at $837. We can sell them for $876, making a profit of $190.

So, although the profits are modest compared to a situation where we had speculated correctly on the directional move of the stock and bought only calls or puts, this way we profit no matter which way the share price moves. The downside to this strategy is that the share price may not move in a big enough way to make profits possible. Remember that extrinsic value will be declining for both the call and the put options.

Selling covered calls against LEAPS and other LEAPS Strategies

A LEAP is a long-term option that is option that expires at a date that is two years in the future. They are regular options otherwise, but you can do some interesting things with LEAPS. Because the expiration date is so far away, they cost a lot more. Looking at Apple, call options with a $195 strike price that expires in two years are selling for $28.28 (for a total price of $2,828). While that seems expensive, consider that 100 shares of Apple would cost $19,422 at the time of writing.

If you buy in the money LEAPS, then you can use them to sell covered calls. This is an interesting strategy that lets you earn a premium income without having to buy the shares of stock.

LEAPS can also be used for other investing strategies. For example, if Apple is trading at $194, we can buy a LEAP option for $3,479 with a strike price of $190 that expires in two years. If, at some point during those two years, the share price rose to $200 we could exercise the option and buy the shares at $190, saving $10 a share. Also, at the same time, we could have been selling covered calls against the LEAPS.

Buying Put Options as Insurance

A put option gives you the right to sell shares of stock at a certain price. Suppose that you wanted to ensure your investment in Apple stock, and you had purchased 100 shares at $191 a share, for a total investment of $19,000. You are worried that the share price is going to drop and so you could buy a put option as a kind of insurance. Looking ahead, you see a put option with a $190 strike price for $4.10. So, you spend $410 and buy the put option.

Should the price of Apple shares suddenly tumble you could exercise your right under the put option to dispose of your shares by selling at the strike price to minimize your losses. Suppose you wake up one morning and the share price has dropped to $170 for some reason. Had you not bought the option you could have tried to get rid of your shares now and take a loss of $21 a share. But, since you bought the put option, you can sell your shares for $190 a share. That is a $1 loss since you purchased the shares at $191. However, you also have to take into account the premium paid for the put options contract, which was $4.10. So, your total loss would be $5.10 a share, but that is still less than the loss of $21 a share that you would have suffered selling the shares on the market at the $170 price. When investors buy stock and a put at the same time, it is called a married put.

Spreads

Spreads involve buying and selling options simultaneously. This is a more complicated options strategy that is only used by advanced traders. You will have to get a high-level designation with your brokerage to use this type of strategy. We won't go into details because these methods are beyond the scope of junior options traders, but we will briefly mention some of the more popular methods so that you can have some awareness.

One of the interesting things about spreads is they can be used by level 3 traders to earn a regular income from options. If you think the price of a stock is going to stay the same or rise, you sell a put credit spread. You sell a higher-priced option and buy a lower-priced option at the same time. The difference in option prices is your profit. There is a chance of loss if the price drops to the strike price of the puts (and you could get assigned if it goes below the strike price of the put option you sold). You can buy back the spread, in that case, to avoid getting assigned.

If you think that the price of a stock is going to drop you can sell to open a credit spread. In this case, you are hoping the price of the stock is going to stay the same or drop. You sell a call with a low strike price and buy a call with a high strike price (both out of the money). The price difference is your profit, and losses are capped.

We can also consider more complicated spreads.

For example, you can use a diagonal spread with calls. This means you buy a call that has a shorter expiration date but a higher strike amount, and then you sell a call with a longer expiration date and a lower strike price. This is done in such a way that you earn more, from selling the call, than you spend on buying the call for a considerable strike amount, and so you get a net credit to your account.

Spreads can become quite complicated, and there are many different types of spreads. If a trader thinks that the price of a stock will only go up a small amount, they can do a bull call spread. Profit and loss are capped in this case. The two options would have the same expiration date.

If you sell a call with a lower strike price and simultaneously buy a call with a high strike price, this is called a bear call spread. You seek to profit if the underlying stock drops in price. This can also be done by using two put options. In that case, you buy a put option that has a higher strike and sell a put option with a lower strike price.

A bull spread involves attempting to profit when the price of the stock rises by a small amount. In this case, you can also use either two call options or two put options. You buy an option with a lower strike price while selling an option with a higher strike price.

Spreads can be combined in more complicated ways. An iron

butterfly combines a bear call spread with a bear puts spread. The purpose of doing this is to generate steady income while minimizing the risk of loss.

An iron condor uses a put spread, and a call spread together. There would be four options simultaneously, with the same expiration dates but different strike prices. It involves selling both sides (calls and puts).

Chapter 5

Application on the Futures Market

What happens when you buy futures? – is one of the most frequent questions in relation to futures trading. The answer to this question can be summarized in a sentence that states: when you buy futures, you are accepting to buy products or services that the company from which you bought futures has not produced yet.

In comparison to stock trading, futures trading is much riskier because you deal with products and services that are not yet produced. With such characteristics, future trading is very popular not only among the producing companies and individuals, and customers but also among speculators as well.

While stocks or shares are being traded on stock markets, futures are being traded on futures markets. The idea of future markets developed from the needs of agricultural producers in the mid-nineteenth century where often happened that the demand was much bigger than supply.

The difference between the futures markets and futures markets today is that today's futures markets have crossed the borders of agricultural production and entered many other sectors such as financial. As such, future markets today are used for buying and selling currencies as well as some other financial instruments. What future markets made possible is the opportunity for a farmer to be able to participate in the goods with customers on the other end of the world. One of the biggest and most important future markets is the International Monetary Market (IMM) that was established in 1972.

Futures are financial derivatives that obtain their value from the movement in the price of another asset. It means that the price of futures is not dependent on its inherent value, but on the price of the asset, the futures contract is tracking.

One of the advantages of the futures market is that is centralized and that people from around the world electronically can make future contracts. These futures contracts will specify the price of the merchandise and the time of delivery. Besides that, every future contract contains information about the quality and the quantity of the sold goods, specific price, and the method in which the goods are to be delivered to the buyers.

A person who buys or sells a futures contract does not pay for the whole value of the contract. He pays a small upfront fee to trigger an open position. For example, if the value of the futures contract is $350,000 when the S&P 500 is 1400, he only pays $21,875 as its initial margin. The exchange sets this margin and may change anytime.

If the S&P 500 moved up to 1500, the futures contract will be worth $375,000. Thus, the person will earn $25,000 in profit. However, if the index fell to 1390 from its original 1400, he will lose $2,500 because the futures contract will now be worth $347,500. This $2,500 is not a realized loss yet. The broker will also not require the individual to add more cash to his trading account.

However, if the index fell to 1300, the futures contract will be worth $325,000. The individual loses $50,000. The broker will require him to add more money to his trading account because his initial margin of $21,875 is no longer enough to cover his losses.

Futures Market Categories

There are similarities in all futures contracts. However, each contract may track different assets. As such, it is important to study the various markets that exist.

You can trade futures contracts on different categories and assets. However, if you are still a new trader, it is important to trade assets that you know. For example, if you are into stock trading for a few years already, you must start with futures contracts using stock indexes. This way, you won't have a hard time understanding the underlying asset. You only need to understand how the futures market works.

After choosing a category, decide on the asset that you want to trade. For example, you want to trade futures contracts in the energy category. Focus on coal, natural gas, crude oil, or heating oil. The markets trade at various levels, so you must understand relevant things, like the nuances, liquidity, margin requirements, contract sizes, and volatility. Do the necessary research before trading in futures contracts.

Types of Trade

A basis trade allows you to go long or short on a futures contract and go short or long on the cash market. It is a wager that the difference in price between the two markets will fluctuate. For example, you decide to buy 10-year US Treasury bond futures then sell a physical 10-year US Treasury bond.

A spread trade allows you to go short and long on two futures contracts. It is a wager that the difference in price between the futures contracts will change. For example, you buy an S&P 500 futures contract for August delivery and sell an S&P 500 futures contract for November delivery.

A hedging trade allows you to sell a futures contract to offset a position you hold in the current market. For example, a stock trader does not want to sell his shares for tax reasons. However, he is fearful of a sharp decline in the stock market so he sells S&P 500 futures contracts as a hedge.

An important issue that must be mention in regards to futures and futures contracts is the notion of prices and the limits of future contracts. In future contracts, prices are expressed in classical currencies such as US dollars. The prices in the aspect of future contracts also have the minimum amount of money for which the price of the product may go up or go down. This minimum in the context of futures contracts is referred to as "ticks".

These tricks are very important for an investor who is investing huge sums of money or is buying a huge number of products because the fluctuation of prices can have an enormous influence on the amount of money spent on certain products. It must also be noted that these "ticks" are not the same for each merchandise. Every commodity in the trading of futures has its own "ticks", the minimum for price fluctuation and it depends on the type of commodity.

How Can We Make a Profit on the Futures Markets?

One thing to remember, is, that even if you buy and sell futures contracts in commodities, you don't take delivery of the underlying commodity. You would close out your contracts before the delivery date.

Let's take a simple example and relate that to a futures contract. You saw a house for sale for $300 000. You believe that in the next year its value will appreciate by about 10% but the downside is you don't have enough money to buy the house outright so you decide to put down a deposit of $30 000. One year later the property has appreciated, as expected, by 10% and is now worth $330 000. You decide to sell the property and make a profit of $30 000. Your initial investment was $30 000 and you sold the house at a profit of $30 000, which gives you a 100% profit on your investment.

Commodity trading works very similarly. Let's take an example. You've been analyzing the corn market and you expect the prices to increase, so you decide to buy the September contract which is presently trading at $2.40 per bushel. There are 5000 bushels in a corn contract. You pay a $500 deposit or margin as required by the exchange.

After four weeks the price has increased to $3.40 a bushel, as expected. This means the contract value is now $3.40 X 5000

= $17000. You bought the contract at $12000 ($2.40 X 5000) four weeks ago and you made a profit of $5000 ($17000 - $14000). The return on your investment of $500 is 1000% in just 4 weeks.

You can also make profits when market prices drop. Let's say you anticipate a drop in the soybeans price from its current level of $5.00 per bushel. There are also 5000 bushels in a soybean contract. You decide to sell one September contract at the current level. You pay a $1000 deposit or margin. Six weeks later the price has dropped considerably, as expected, to $3.50 per bushel. You decide to close your position and take your profits. You do this by buying a contract to offset the contract you sold six weeks earlier. The difference between the price you sold and the price bought back is your profit. $25000($5.00 X 5000) − $17500($3.5 X 5000) = $7500 profit for an investment of $1000. 750% profit in six weeks.

Selling Short - How does it work?

How can one make money when the market is dropping? This is something that happens around us every day of our lives. Let's say you are a car dealer and you sell brand new cars. The factory-supplied you with a couple of cars on consignment that you can display on your showroom floor and you don't have to pay for them right away because the factory allows you some time to sell them. After a while, you sell one of the cars for $50 000 and now you have to pay the factory, but only $30 000, which is the cost price to you that leaves you with a profit of $20 000. What did you actually do? You borrowed the car from the factory and sold it to your client at a higher price than the factory charges you and that way you made money. You sold first and bought it later. When we sell futures, we do the same thing, we sell high because we anticipate the market will trade down and we can buy back or close our position at a lower price and make a profit. Just like the car dealer.

There Must Be Risks?

With any business you have risks. When you open a business, you have to invest huge amounts of capital upfront to set up your business. You have to rent offices, buy stock and pay salaries, etc. before the first customer walks through your door. You have no idea how many customers will walk in or whether you will generate enough business to even recover your capital expenses. With the speculative markets it's the same but how you manage your risk will determine your success. Let's compare the stock market with the futures market, you can diversify your risk in the stock market by investing in different non-correlated stock and under normal circumstances, it will work well but sudden political changes or news regarding the economy can affect all share prices overnight, even if you did spread your investments across several companies, all your profits can be wiped in extreme situations, as we have seen in recent years.

Comparing this to futures markets where you can spread your investments across a diverse range of commodity markets like corn, silver, oil, sugar, wheat, or cotton, it's impossible to imagine any situation affecting all these markets at the same time. Economic disasters, droughts, war, floods, and political events will always happen and they also affect certain commodity markets but spreading your investment not only minimizes your losses but also puts you in a position to benefit from any price move.

Chapter 6

Which Market to Trade and with which Broker

There is a huge array of products to trade with on offer but for scalping you need products with large volumes exchanged and volatility. I find these in the mini DAX and the e-mini Dow futures. The volatility, *i.e.* daily range (distance between the low of the day and the high of the day) is wide. In addition, and this point is very important, these products are traded on regulated and centralized markets: Eurex for the DAX futures and CME for the e-mini Dow; as opposed to CFDs which are OTC products; *i.e.* your broker is the counterpart of your trade. When you buy, your broker is your seller and when you sell, your broker is buying from you. On the other hand, on a centralized market, your order is routed and executed when someone else's order matches yours (buyers' and sellers' prices meet). Also, in the future markets, you can see the volume of transactions, while on the CFD, your broker may show no volume at all or only the volumes exchanged on their platform.

And more importantly, in future markets, you see the prices offered by other market participants while on CFDs, you only get the prices offered by your broker. To illustrate, this I have just taken below a snapshot of prices offered by two different CFD brokers at the same time.

Ticket order

Which broker offers the right price?

In case of high volatility, CFDs do not react the same way as futures: the prices may adjust at a different pace and the spread offered by the broker may increase. A market order may even be repriced if the market is moving very quickly. Stop orders may incur slippage which means you will lose few points to your broker as the price you are paid is few points away from your stop order.

I like to compare CFDs and futures to the current trends in grocery consumption. People like to consume fresh products that come directly from the farm, without any middlemen and wholesalers that make their margin in the process. Well, trading futures is similar. You get the prices directly from the market while CFDs are products offered by your broker who gets their revenue through the spreads. Moreover, CFD providers hedge their positions or some part of them using futures and options.

So, I can only recommend that you trade with future or mini future contracts. However, CFDs can be useful to trade small positions when you make your first steps in trading as you can trade products at only one euro per point instead of 5 euros on a mini future contract or even 25 euros per point on the DAX future. Note that CFDs are not available in all countries due to local laws and financial regulations.

But if you can and want to trade CFDs, make sure you look at the spreads offered by different brokers before choosing who to trade with. Half a point is not much different, but in scalping, it means a lot. After 20 trades, paying half a point more on each trade at one euro per point will result in an extra 10 euros wasted in commissions; and so on, after 40 trades, you will have wasted 20 euros. Let's say in a month if you perform 600 to 800 trades, you will then have wasted 300 to 400 euros in extra commissions.

How to choose your broker:

In order to be able to scalp in good conditions, you need to look out for the following points when choosing your broker:

- Tight spreads if you choose to work with CFDs. One euro or dollar per point is the maximum you should pay as you don't want to be working just for your broker;

- Real-time data flux is essential. The subscription to the Eurex data flux (DAX and mini DAX) will cost you about 20 euros per month and another 25 euros for a subscription to CME CBOT (e-mini Dow) data. Your broker collects the fees for the data supplier; you don't need to pay the supplier directly. If you just want to trade CFDs you won't have to pay these fees, but you will have only access to the data provided by your broker.

- Most of the platforms will let you place simple orders such as buy limit or sell limit orders, with the option to set up an automated take profit and stop-loss orders. But some go even further by letting you set up an automated order for part of the position and another one for the second part of the position and so on if you want to set up 3 different targets. I

- Be aware that some brokers operate with a first in first out rule which means that they won't let you have opposite positions on the same product run separately, a.k.a. hedging. A new executed sell order may not open a position but offset or close an already opened buy position. On the other hand, CFD brokers may let you trade, hedge, and operate your positions separately from one another. While short and long positions of equivalent quantities and on the same product offset each other in

  theory, your broker may still calculate a margin cover for each position separately. So, keep an eye on your margin usage.

- If you are starting with a small account, *i.e.* with less than € 5,000 look for brokers that will let you trade on small quantities, as small as 1/100th of one lot. That way you can start trading taking minimum risk until you build confidence in your trading.

- Being able to trade from a smartphone, an iPad, or similar. I certainly cannot recommend that you use these devices for your scalping, but they shall be used as part of plan B if a problem comes up with your computer while you are trading or if your internet broadband suddenly shuts down or resets itself. Your smartphone connected to a mobile phone network will be your backup device to modify or close some orders if necessary, until your computer and the internet are back up and running. Most brokers offer mobile technology in today's world.

- This was the plan B. The plan C is that you should be able to call your broker's trading desk as a last resort, in case of emergency, if your computer and your mobile application don't let you perform an action that needs to be done.

- Lastly, you absolutely need to work with a

minimum of two brokers because if for any reason there is a technical problem on one of your brokers' platforms, you need to able to act swiftly on your second broker's platform. Let's say you need to close a position but broker A's platform for some reason is not working. Then you can always open an opposite order on the broker's B platform. For instance, you need to close a long position with broker A, but a technical problem doesn't let you do so. Then you should open a short position with broker B until everything is back up and running. Then you can work on closing these positions simultaneously afterward.

Once you are ready to trade with the mini futures, I recommend that you have at least 12,000 euros to be able to scalp with 2 lots when the occasion occurs. For the most accurate information, choose the tick-by-tick data flux if you can choose a data provider. Some data providers offer market data sent to your computer on a second by second basis while others have their data refreshed on a tick by tick basis, which is every time a transaction occurs on the market, showing you the latest price exchanged.

You may want to explore and trade some additional markets, but I recommend not trading more than two markets at a time

because scalping requires concentration and prompt action in your trades.

Chapter 7

Application on the Stocks Market

A stock is a form of security that suggests proportional ownership in a company. Stocks are acquired and sold predominantly on stock exchanges, however, there can be private arrangements as well. These exchanges/trades need to fit within government laws which are expected to shield investors from misleading practices. Stocks can be obtained from a large number of online platforms.

Businesses issue (offer) stock to raise capital. The holder of stock (a shareholder) has now acquired a portion of the company and shares its profit and loss. Therefore, a a shareholder is considered an owner of the company.

Ownership is constrained by the number of shares an individual owns regarding the number of shares the company is divided into. For example, if a company has 1,000 shares of stock and one individual owns 100 shares, that individual would receive 10% of the company's capital and profits.

Financial experts don't own companies as such; instead, they sell shares offered by companies. Under the law, there are different types of companies and some are viewed as independent because of how they have set up their businesses. Regardless of the type of company, ultimately, they must report costs, income, changes in structure, etc., or they can be sued. A business set up as an "independent," known as a sole proprietorship, suggests that the owner assumes all responsibilities and is liable for all financial aspects of the business. A business set up as a company of any sort means that the business is separate from its owners and the owners aren't personally responsible for the financial aspects of the business.

This separation is of extreme importance; it limits the commitment of both the company and the shareholder/owner. If the business comes up short, a judge may rule for the company to be liquidated – however, your very own assets will not come under threat. The court can't demand that you sell your shares, though the value of your shares will have fallen significantly.

Trading is the basic idea of exchanging one thing for another. In this regard, it is buying or selling, where compensation is paid by a buyer to a seller. Trade can happen inside an economy among sellers and buyers. Overall, trade allows countries to develop markets for the exchange of goods and services that for the most part wouldn't have been available otherwise. It is the reason why an American purchaser can choose between a Japanese, German, or American conduit. Due to overall trade, the market contains progressively significant competition which makes it possible for buyers to get products and services at affordable costs.

In fiscal markets, trading implies the buying and selling of insurances, for instance, the purchase of stock on the New York Stock Exchange (NYSE).

Fundamentals of stock/securities exchange

The exchange of stocks and securities happens on platforms like the New York Stock Exchange and Nasdaq. Stocks are recorded on a specific exchange, which links buyers and sellers, allowing them to trade those stocks. The trade is tracked in the market and allows buyers to get company stocks at fair prices. The value of these stocks moves – up or down – depending on many factors in the market. Investors can look at these factors and decide on whether or not they want to purchase these stocks.

A market record tracks the value of a stock, which either addresses the market with everything considered or a specific fragment of the market. You're likely going to hear most about the S&P 500, the Nasdaq composite, and the Dow Jones Industrial Average in this regard.

Financial advisors use data to benchmark the value of their portfolios and, some of the time, to shed light on their stock exchanging decisions. You can also put your assets into an entire portfolio based on the data available in the market.

Stock exchanging information

Most financial experts would be well-taught to build a portfolio with a variety of different financial assets. However, experts who prefer a greater degree of movement take more interest in the stock exchange. This type of investment incorporates the buying and selling of stocks.

The goal of people who trade in stock is to use market data and things happening in the market to either sell the stock for a profit or buy stocks at low prices to make a profit later. Some stock traders are occasional investors, which means they buy and sell now and then. Others are serious investors, making as little as twelve exchanges for every month.

Financial experts who exchange stocks do wide research, as often as possible, devoting hours day by day tracking the market. They rely upon particular audits, using instruments to chart a stock's advancements attempting to find trading openings and examples. Various online middlemen offer stock exchanging information, including expert reports, stock research, and charting tools.

What is a bear market?

A bear market means stock prices are falling — limits move to 20% or more — based on data referenced previously.

Progressive financial experts may be alright with the term bear market. Profiting in the trade business will always far outlast the typical bear market; which is why in a bear market, smart investors will hold their shares until the market recovers. This has been seen time and time again. The S&P 500, which holds around 500 of the greatest stocks in the U.S., has consistently maintained an average of around 7% consistently when you factor in reinvested profits and varied growth. That suggests that if you invested $1,000 30 years ago, you could have around $7,600 today.

Stock market crash versus a correction

A crash happens when the commercial value prices fall by 10% or more. It is an unexpected, incredibly sharp fall in stock prices; for example, in October 1987, when stocks dove 23%

in a single day.

The stock market tends to be affected longer by crashes in the market and can last from two to nine years.

The criticalness of improvement

You can't avoid the possibility of bear markets or the economy crashing, or even losing money while trading. What you can do, however, is limit the effects these types of the market will have on your investment by maintaining a diversified portfolio.

Diversification shields your portfolio from unavoidable market risks. If you dump a large portion of your cash into one means of investment, you're betting on growth that can rapidly turn to loss by a large number of factors.

To cushion risks, financial specialists expand by pooling different types of stocks together, offsetting the inevitable possibility that one stock will crash and your entire portfolio will be affected or you lose everything.

You can put together individual stocks and assets in a single portfolio. One recommendation: dedicate 10% or less of your portfolio to a few stocks you believe in each time you decide to invest.

Ways to invest

There are different ways for new investors to purchase stocks. If you need to pay very low fees, you will need to invest additional time making your own trades. If you wish to beat the market, however, you'll pay higher charges by getting someone to trade on your behalf. If you don't have the time or interest, you may need to make do with lower results.

Most stock purchasers get anxious when the market is doing well. Incredibly, this makes them purchase stocks when they are the most volatile. Obviously, business share that is not performing well triggers fear. That makes most investors sell when the costs are low.

Choosing what amount to invest is an individual decision. It depends upon your comfort with risk. It depends upon your ability and capacity to invest energy into getting some answers concerning the stock exchange.

Purchase Stocks Online

Purchasing stocks online costs, the least, yet gives little encouragement. You are charged a set price, or a percent of your purchase, for every trade. It very well may be the least secure. It expects you to teach yourself altogether on the best way to invest. Consequently, it additionally takes the most time. It's a smart idea to check the top web-based trading sites before you begin.

Investment Groups

Joining an investment group gives you more data at a sensible price. However, it takes a great deal of effort to meet with the other group members. They all have different degrees of expertise. You might be required to pool a portion of your assets into a group account before trading. Once more, it's a smart idea to examine the better investment groups before you begin.

Full-time Brokers

A full-time broker is costly because you'll pay higher fees. Nevertheless, you get more data and assistance and that shields you from greed and fear. You should search around to choose a decent broker that you can trust. The Securities and Trade Commission shares helpful tips on the best ways to choose a broker.

Money Manager

Money managers select and purchase the stocks for you. You pay them a weighty charge, typically 1-2 percent of your complete portfolio. If the chief progresses admirably, it takes a minimal amount of time. That is because you can simply meet with them more than once per year. Ensure you realize how to choose a decent financial advisor.

File Fund

Otherwise called market traded assets, record assets can be a cheap and safe approach to benefit from stocks. They essentially track the stocks in a file. Models incorporate the MSCI developing business sector record. The reserve rises and falls alongside the file. There is no yearly cost. However, it's difficult to outflank the market along these lines since record supports just track the market. All things being equal, there is a great deal of valid justifications for why you ought to put resources into a file fund.

Common Funds

Common assets are a generally more secure approach to benefit from stocks. The company supervisor will purchase a gathering of stocks for you. You don't possess the stock, yet a portion of the investment. Most assets have a yearly cost, between 0.5 percent to 3 percent. They guarantee to outflank the S&P 500, or other equivalent file reserves. For additional information, see 16 Best Tips on Mutual Fund Basics and Before You Buy a Mutual Fund.

Theories of stock investments

Theories of stock investments look like basic resources. Both of them pool all of their investors' dollars into one viably supervised hold. In any case, theories stock investments put assets into ensnared fiscal instruments known as subordinates. They guarantee to win the normal resources with these significantly used theories.

Theoretical stock investments are private companies, not open organizations. That suggests they aren't coordinated by the SEC. They are risky, yet various investors acknowledge this higher danger prompts a better yield.

Selling Your Stocks

As important as buying stocks is knowing when to sell them. Most financial experts buy when the stock exchange is rising and sell when it's falling. Regardless, a clever money marketer seeks after a strategy subject to their financial needs.

You should reliably watch out for the noteworthy market records. The three greatest U.S. records are the Dow Jones Industrial Average, the S&P 500, and the Nasdaq. In any case, don't solidify in case they enter a modification or a mishap. Those events don't prop up long.

Chapter 8

How Does The Stock Market Work?

The stock market is not like your neighborhood grocery store: you can only buy and sell through licensed brokers who make trades on major indexes like NASDAQ and S&P 100. This is where investors meet up to buy and sell stocks or other financial investments like bonds. The stock market is made up of so many exchanges, like the NASDAQ or the New York Exchange. These exchanges are not open all through the day. Most exchanges like the NASDAQ and NYSE are open from 9:30 am to 4 pm. EST. Although premarket and trading after closing time now exist, not all brokers do this.

Companies list their stocks on an exchange in a bid to raise money for their business, and investors buy those shares. In addition to this, investors can trade shares among themselves, and the exchange keeps track of the rate of supply and demand of each listed stock. The rate of supply and demand for stocks determines the price. If there's a high demand for a particular stock, its price tends to rise. On the other hand, the price of a stock goes down when there's less demand for it. The stock market computer algorithm handles these varying fluctuations in prices.

How Does The Stock Market Work?

A Stock market analysis definitely looks like gibberish to beginners and average investors. However, you should know that the way this market works is actually quite simple. Just imagine a typical auction house or an online auction website. This market works in the same way - it allows buyers and sellers to negotiate prices and carry out successful trades. The first stock market took place in a physical marketplace, however, these days, trades happen electronically via the internet and online stockbrokers. From the comfort of your homes, you can easily bid and negotiate for the prices of stocks with online stockbrokers.

Furthermore, you might come across news headlines that say the stock market has crashed or gone up. Once again, don't fret or get all excited when you come across such news. Most often than not, this means a stock market index has gone up or down. In other words, the stocks in a market index have gone down. Before we proceed, let's explore the meaning of market indexes.

Stock Market Indexes

Market indexes track the performance of a group of stocks in a particular sector like manufacturing or technology. The value of the stocks featured in an index is representative of all the stocks in that sector. It is very important to take note of what stocks each market index represents. In addition to this, giant market indexes like the Dow Jones Industrial Average, the NASDAQ composite, and the Standard & Poor's 500, are often used as proxies for the performance of the stock market as a whole. You can choose to invest in an entire index through the exchange-traded funds and index funds, as it can track a specific sector or index of the stock market.

Bullish and Bearish Markets

Talking about the bullish outlook of the stock market is guaranteed to get beginners looking astonished. Yes, it sounds ridiculous at first, but with time, you get to appreciate the ingenuity of these descriptions. Let's start with the bearish market. A bear is an animal you would never want to meet on a hike; it strikes fear into your heart, and that's the effect you will get from a bearish market. The threshold for a bearish market varies within a 20 percent loss or more.

Most young investors unfamiliar with a bear market as we've been in a bull market since the first quarter of 2019. In fact, this makes it the second-longest bull market in history. Just as you have probably guessed by now, a bull market indicates that stock prices are rising. You should know that the market is continually changing from bull to bear and vice versa. From the Great Recession to the global market crash, these changing market prices indicate the start of larger economic patterns. For instance, a bull market shows that investors are investing heavily and that the economy is doing extremely well. On the other hand, a bear market shows investors are scared and pulling back, with the economy on the brink of collapsing. If this made you paranoid about the next bear market, don't fret. Business analysts have shown that the average bull market generally outlasts the average bear market by a large margin. This is why you can grow your money in stocks over an extended period of time.

Stock Market Corrections and Crash

A stock market crash is every investor's nightmare. It is usually extremely difficult to watch stocks that you've spent so many years accumulating diminish before your very eyes. Yes, this is how volatile the stock market is. Stock market crashes usually include a very sudden and sharp drop in stock prices, and it might herald the beginning of a bear market. On the other hand, stock market corrections occur when the market drops by 10 percent - this is just the market's way of balancing itself. The current bull market has gone through 5 market corrections.

Analyzing the Stock Market

You are not psychic. It is nearly impossible to accurately predict the outcome of your stock to the last detail. However, you can become near perfect at reading the stock market by learning how to properly analyze the components of this market. There are two basic types of analyses: technical analysis and fundamental analysis.

Fundamental Market Analysis

Fundamental analysis involves getting data about a company's stocks or a particular sector in the stock market, via financial records, company assets, economic reports, and market share. Analysts and investors can conduct fundamental analysis via the metrics on a corporation's financial statement. These metrics include cash flow statements, balance sheet statements, footnotes, and income statements. Most times, you can get a company's financial statement through a 10-k report in the database. In addition to this, the SEC's EDGAR is a good place to get the financial statement of the company you are interested in. With the financial statement, you can deduce the revenues, expenses, and profits a company has made.

What's more? By looking at the financial statement, you will have a measure of a company's growth trajectory, leverage, liquidity, and solvency. Analysts utilize different ratios to make an accurate prediction about stocks. For example, the quick ratio and current ratio are useful in determining if a company will be able to pay its short-term liabilities with the current asset. If the current ratio is less than 1, the company is in poor financial health and may not be able to recover from its short-term debt. Here's another example: a stock analyst can use the debt ratio to measure the current level of debt taken on by the company. If the debt ratio is above 1, it means the company has more debt than assets and it's only a matter of time before it goes under.

Technical Market Analysis

This is the second part of stock market analysis and it revolves around studying past market actions to predict the stock price direction. Technical analysts put more focus on the price and volume of shares. Additionally, they analyze the market as a whole and study the supply and demand factors that dictate market movement. In technical analyses, charts are of inestimable value. Charts are a vital tool as they show the graphical representation of a stock's trend within a set time frame. What's more? Technical investors are able to identify and mark certain areas as resistance or support levels on a chart. The resistance level is a previous high stock price before the current price. On the other hand, support levels are represented by a previous low before the current stock price. Therefore, a break below the support levels marks the beginning of a bearish trend. Alternatively, a break above the resistance level marks the beginning of a bullish market trend. Technical analysis is only effective when the rise and fall of stock prices are influenced by supply and demand forces. However, technical analysis is mostly rendered ineffective in the face of outside forces that affect stock prices such as stock splits, dividend announcements, scandals, changes in management, mergers, and so on. Investors can make use of both types of analyses to get an accurate prediction of their stock values.

Why You Need To Diversify

According to research by Ned Davis, a bear market occurs every 3.5 years and has an average lifespan of 15 months. One thing is clear, though: you can't avoid bear markets. You can, however, avoid the risks that come with investing in a single investment portfolio. Let's look at a common mistake that new investors typically make. Research points to the fact that individual stocks dwindle to a loss of 100 percent. By throwing in your lot with one company, you are exposing yourself to many setbacks. For example, you can lose your money if a corporation is embroiled in a scandal, poor leadership, and regulatory issues. So, how can you balance out your losses? By investing in a therefore mentioned index fund or ETF fund, as these indexes hold many different stocks, as by doing this, you've automatically diversified your investment. Here's a nugget to cherish: put 90 percent of your investment funds in an index fund, and put the remaining 10 percent in an individual stock that you trust.

When to Sell Your Stocks

One thing is sure - you are not going to hold your stocks forever. All our investment advice and energies are directed towards buying. Yes, it is the buying of stocks that kick-start the whole investment when chasing your dream concept. However, just as every beginning has an end, you will eventually sell every stock you buy. It is the natural order. Even so, selling off stock is not an easy decision. Heck! It's even harder to determine the right time to sell. This is the point where greed and human emotions start to battle with pragmatism. Many investors try to make sensible selling decisions solely based on price movements. However, this is not a sure strategy, as it is still sensible to hold onto a stock that has fallen in value. Conversely, selling a stock when it has reached your target is seen as prudent. So, how can you navigate around this dilemma?

Why Selling Is So Hard

Do you know why it's so hard to let go of your stocks even when you have a fixed strategy to follow? The answer lies in human greed. When making decisions, it's an innate human tendency to be greedy.

Chapter 9

Application on the Forex Market

Trading Platforms

If there's something essentially needed to trade Forex, it is a trading platform! If you are assuming that trading is ideal for absolute beginners, I'd say yes, but you are not going to make millions overnight. If you look at Forex trading like gambling, you will not be able to become a profitable trader because greed will invade you. If you want to become a great trader, you must have skills and patience. Also, you must keep practicing trading as it helps to shape up your trading style into a better version. Once you do your homework, you'd feel as if you are good to go. But then, Forex trading knowledge can't be accumulated into a few pages or days. It is a continuous learning process. If you have just started with the basics of Forex trading, you have a lot more to learn. A beginner should have access to a user-friendly platform that can be easily handled when trading.

A beginner's journey is already complex, so when the trader doesn't select the right platform, the difficulties increase. When the trading platform is easy to understand, you will not have difficulties when trying out new strategies and techniques on the demo account. There are many reliable brokers that you can select when you are trading Forex, but the problem is finding the ideal broker. To earn extra income, Forex is a good choice. But it doesn't mean Forex can be traded as the main source of income. However, either main income or part-time income, you must find the ideal broker and an excellent platform to keep going in trading. Even though there are many good brokers, you must do your research to find the right one that offers the most straightforward trading platform. I know, you will encounter difficulties when selecting the right broker, so let me help you. Before you settle for an ideal platform check whether the platform is reliable; it is one of the most crucial factors that you must consider when selecting a trading platform. You don't want to lose all the money that you collected, so make sure to find a platform that you can rely on. If you're going to deposit and withdraw your cash without facing any issues, the trading platform must be reliable.

Another important factor is charges related to the platform. You must consider the charges because your profits will disappear even before you know it if the charges are high.

Besides, you are just starting your journey so your income will not be massive. The smaller income that you gain must be protected, so for that, you must consider the charges related to the trading platform.

You must next consider the licensing factor of the Forex platforms. If the relevant authorities monitor the platform, they are unlikely to fool you. The trading platforms will work according to terms and conditions, so you don't have to worry when you are trading through them. But to find whether the platform is licensed, you must do some research even if it is tough. Along with these, you must consider the simplicity of the Forex trading platform, but due to the software used, eventually, almost all the trading platforms have become easier to handle. In the meantime, don't forget to consider the leverage, margin, and other requirements that generally should be considered when selecting a trading platform. Once you select the ideal platform, you will be able to trade in a hassle-free way. However, there's more to learn about Forex trading platforms. So, keep reading!

There are two types of platforms, such as commercial and prop platforms. Before you pick any, you must ensure to understand the types in detail. Thus, prop platforms are designed by Forex brokers, and specialized companies develop commercial platforms. However, there are unique features for both trading platforms. Even though the prop platforms are considerable, there are times when you might want to change the broker. But when you try to do it, you have to learn the new platform from scratch.

Basically, prop platforms are not suitable for naïve traders because you might have to struggle a lot to understand the sophisticated features. But, why do these trading platforms include complex features? Well, a Forex broker's main duty is not to create and manage trading platforms. Hence, they don't spend much time introducing better trading tools and features to prop platforms. For example, if you consider Aplari or FXCM you might find it difficult to handle because brokers develop these. Beginners like you need a lot of time to get adjusted to the trading platform. But, I don't say trade execution speed is terrible because it is excellent in prop platforms, yet beginners will have a tough time understanding this platform.

So, beginners like you can consider the platforms designed by professional companies. One of the most common trading software is Metatrader. This is a user-friendly and high-standard platform that you can consider even if you don't have experience. But if you are looking for a platform that includes broker feeds, then this is not going to help because the commercial platform has poor customization. These companies sell commercial platforms to Forex brokers so the benefits may be biased towards the broker, but not the trader.

Yet, as beginners, you are not going to find anything better than commercial platforms because they are extremely user-friendly and flexible.

So that's about the types of platforms that you will come across. But, I'm pretty sure you'll have some doubts related to selecting the right trading platform. Hence, I'll solve some of the common questions below.

What to consider when selecting the right platform?

You already know this, yet let me provide a brief answer. But, before you decide, it is better to read some reviews about the platform so that you will make a solid decision.

Which Forex software will be ideal?

A technical trader must consider a comfortable charting platform. The platform that you have selected must have all the necessary tools. Only if you select the right trading platform will you be able to enjoy trading. A fundamental trader must consider the news and analysis factor and check whether it is accessible by the Forex software that the trader has selected.

Should you trust the platforms that provide exclusive offers?

You already know when something is too good to be true, we shouldn't rely on it. Just like that, if a platform is providing exclusive things that you cannot fathom, then you must think twice before considering that platform. If they are offering so much, they should have massive profits. If yes, then from where do they get so much profit? Instead of falling for exclusive offers, you can find a platform that is reliable and reasonable.

I hope these questions and answers cleared most doubts that you had about trading platforms. However, it is better to get some idea about the famous trading platforms. Let's get started!

MetaTrader 5

Both MT4 and MT5 were introduced by one company some time back. The best thing about MetaTrader 5 is that you can use it to trade options and stock trading. Most traders who trade on the stock market along with the Forex market consider MT5 because it is simple and beneficial.

MetaTrader 4

Currently, a higher percentage of traders use MetaTrader 4 to trade Forex. Even brokers recommend MT4 as the best trading platform. Yet, certain fund managers and professional traders don't prefer MT4. Beginners like you can benefit immensely from this platform because it is user-friendly. If you have selected the right broker who offers MT4, you will be able to enjoy comparatively cheap prices. Also, this is an old platform provided to Forex traders. You must also note that this platform has a great team to solve issues related to trading. But sadly, fund managers believe that trade execution is not as fast as they want.

NinjaTrader

This is the oldest platform remaining in the industry. Even now, some traders prefer using this trading platform because it is easy to handle. Also, this platform has special features that can be enjoyed by traders.

TradeStation

This is for fund managers and professional traders because this platform has the speed and high-end technology required by professional traders and managers. This platform has some issues with the user-friendly option, but fund managers and professional traders don't worry about it.

Finally, you must understand that the trading platform is all about how comfortable you are with the platform. It should provide an easy path to enter and exit trades while providing a user-friendly feature. If you select the right platform, you will be able to make a solid trading decision. But, making profits will depend on your skill, so you can't entirely depend on the trading platform. Of course, it is a supporting factor, but it is not a reason to make profits. If you want to reach success in trading, you must not think twice to get help from Forex mentors and professionals. Anyway, let me provide some insights into some other factors as well.

Opening an Account

You must be excited about Forex trading. But, without learning the ways to open an account, how will you even trade? With online Forex trading, the excitement to trade Forex has increased immensely. However, to start trading Forex, you must find a broker, select a trading platform, and then open an account. But the part of opening an account is pretty easy. To open an account, you need certain things including name, email, address, contact number, account type, a password for the account, citizenship, date of birth, employment details, Tax ID, and a few more financial questions. The steps of opening an account will differ from one broker to another, yet the following are the general procedures to open an account:

Sometimes, you might have to fill the application with the details related to the trading experience.

Select the broker and check for a suitable and available account.

After completing the application, register with your username, and then you'll receive the credentials to your Forex trading account. Now, you'll have access to the broker's client portal and then, transfer the deposit funds through any of the possible payment methods to your trading account. But remember, you might have to bear charges as per the payment method.

Once the funding procedure is complete, you can then trade Forex. But, your broker will provide necessary guidance and ideas before you enter into live trading.

Once you complete these procedures, you are good to begin your journey. But, are you wondering why you have to follow all these hectic rules and regulations? Well, the Forex market wasn't filled with rules and regulations, but once the market allowed retail trading, the rules and regulations became compulsory. If the market wasn't strict, it would be easy for the market participants to gamble on the market. The factor of reliability will become questionable. Also, you will not find brokers who don't require these details. On the other hand, if you find brokers who don't ask these questions, then you have to think about opening an account.

Well, an important thing about opening an account is risk disclosure. As a beginner, you are likely to be mindless about this factor, but remember, this is very important.

Conclusion

Thank you for making it through to the end of *Day Trading Strategies*, let's hope it was informative and able to provide you with all of the tools and information you need to manage your journey in the market trade.

Day trading is described as the process of speculation of risks and either buying or selling financial instruments on the same day of trading. The financial instruments are bought at a lower price and later sold at a higher price. People who participate in this form of trade are mostly referred to as speculators. Day trading is a different form of trading known as swing trading. Swing trading involves selling financial instruments and latter buying them at a lower price. It is a form of trade that has several people have invested their time and capital in. The potential for making profits is very high. However, it is also accompanied by the high potential of making huge percentages of loss. People who are terms as high-risk takers have the potential to realize good amounts of profits or huge losses. It is because of the nature of the trade. The losses are experienced because of several variables that are always present in trading. The gains and individual experiences are brought to light by margin buying.

There is a big difference between swing trade and day trade. The difference hails from their definitions, it goes a mile ahead to time spent in and risks involved in both forms of trade. Day trade has lower risk involvement but one has to spend more of his or her time, unlike swing trade. Day traders are prone to participating in two forms of trade which are long trades or short trades. Long trade involves an individual purchasing the financial instruments and selling them after them increasing in value. On the other hand, short trade involves selling financial instruments and later purchasing them after their prices have dropped.

The trading market has undergone through several advancements. The major change was witnessed during the deregulation process. There was the creation of electronic financial markets during this period. One of the major innovations was the high-frequency trading index. It uses heavy algorithms to enable huge financial firms in stock trading to perform numerous orders in seconds. It is advantageous because it can also predict market trends.

The process of day trading has several challenges. An individual is supposed to be able to make a good decision during two important moments. The first moment is during a good streak and the other is during moments an individual has a poor run. At this point risk management and trading, psychology comes in handy to help an individual in the trade.

One is not supposed to panic or make hasty decisions during these moments. An individual need to have an effective watchlist. A good watchlist built by a trader is supposed to be able to understand the modern trading markets. This is made possible when it features stocks in play, float and market capital, pre-market grippers, real-time intraday scans, and planning trade based on scanners. The success of day trading is also incumbent on effective strategies. The common strategies include ABCD patterns, bag flag momentum, reversal trading, movie average trading, and opening range breakouts.

There are also advanced strategies that can be used to ensure the success of day trading. Three of these strategies are one stock in play, bull flag, and a fallen angel. With the use of these strategies, a successful trader builds his or her trading business step by step. The common steps involve building a watchlist, having a trading plan, and knowing how to execute.